INDIAN PRAIRIE PUBLIC LIBRARY DISTRICT

3 1946 00382 7018

NOV 1 4 2006

D1283617

INDIAN PRAIRIE PUBLIC LIBRARY
401 Plainfield Road
Darien, IL 60561

Smell it!

Sally Hewitt

QEB Publishing, Inc.

INDIAN PRAIRIE PUBLIC LIBRARY
401 Plainfield Road
Darien, IL 60561

Copyright © QEB Publishing, Inc. 2005

First published in the United States by
QEB Publishing, Inc.
23062 La Cadena Drive
Laguna Hills, CA 92653

www.qeb–publishing.com

All rights reserved. No part of this
publication may be reproduced, stored
in a retrieval system, or transmitted in
any form or by any means, electronic,
mechanical, photocopying, recording, or
otherwise, without the prior permission of
the publisher, nor be otherwise circulated
in any form of binding or cover other
than that in which it is published and
without a similar condition being
imposed on the subsequent purchaser.

Library of Congress Control Number:
2005921172

ISBN 1-59566-088-7

Written by Sally Hewitt

Series Consultant Sally Morgan
Project Editor Honor Head
Series Designer Zeta Jones
Photographer Michael Wicks
Picture Researcher Nic Dean

Publisher Steve Evans
Creative Director Louise Morley
Editorial Manager Jean Coppendale

Printed and bound in China

Picture credits

Corbis/Norbert Schaefer 5 /Bill Stormont
6, /Julie Houck 14, /Tom Stewart 15, /Rick
Gayle Studio 15, /Walter Smith 16, /Paul
Barton 17, /David Thomas 18, /Ariel
Skelley 18, /Wolfgang Kaehler 20;

Getty Images/Britt Erlanson/Stone
7, /Billy Hustace/Photographer's Choice
9, /James Darell/Stone 10, /BoThomas/
Stone 14, /Scott VanDyke/Beateworks 19
(background), /Cousteau Society/The
Image Bank 20.

The words in bold **like this** are explained in the Glossary on page 22.

Contents

Smell this   4

Smelly warnings   6

A good sniff!   8

Stuffy nose   10

What's that smell?   12

Clean and dirty   14

Outdoor smells   16

Indoor smells   18

Animals and smell   20

Glossary   22

Index   23

Parents' and teachers' notes   24

Smell this

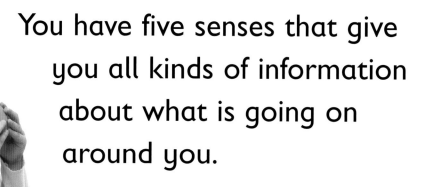

You have five senses that give you all kinds of information about what is going on around you.

The five senses are sight, touch, taste, smell, and hearing. This book is about your sense of smell.

Your sense of smell helps you enjoy your food.

This flower smells nice.

There are smells all around you. What can you smell now?

Most flowers look pretty and smell nice. What smells do you like?

A dirty dishcloth looks horrid and smells horrid! What smells don't you like?

Smelly warnings

You often don't think about smells unless they are very strong. But smells can give you important warnings.

Smoke has a very strong smell. The smell of smoke can be a warning. It makes you think of danger. Is something on fire?

◀ Firefighters wear masks to protect their noses and mouths from smoke.

A bad smell warns
you when something
could harm you.

Rotten food smells
bad so you don't
want to eat it!

YUM!
Smells
good!

Most food smells
delicious and helps
you to feel hungry.

A good sniff!

When you **sniff** deeply, smells in the air go up holes in your **nose** called **nostrils**.

Tiny hairs at the back of your nose sense the smells and send a message to your brain. Your brain tells you what you are smelling.

That smells tasty.

Dogs have a much stronger sense of smell than you. They can smell things you can't.

Police use **sniffer dogs** to help them find things.

Activity

Put some smelly cheese (or anything with a strong smell) on a plate. Ask a friend to hide it in a room.

Can you find the smelly cheese by sniffing it out?

Stuffy nose

When you have a cold your nose gets stuffed up. Smells can't go up your nose, so you can't smell very well.

You probably don't mind not being able to smell bad smells!

◄ When your nose is blocked, you also miss smelling good smells.

If you have a cold, you may not be able to smell food properly. This means you might not feel very hungry.

Activity

Make a list of things you often smell. Which smells would you miss if you had a stuffy nose?

	Would miss	Wouldn't miss
Hamburgers	✔	
Toothpaste		✔
Soap	✔	
Dirty socks		✔
Chocolate	✔	
Oranges	✔	

What's that smell?

Your brain remembers smells you have smelled before. The first time you smell a new smell, it seems very strong and you notice it immediately.

You have to see what is making the new smell to know what it is. When you smell it again, you remember it.

I know that smel

It's harder to recognize a smell when you can't see what it is coming from.

Put some lemon slices, chocolate, cheese, soap, toothpaste, and hand lotion into 6 plastic cups. Cover the cups with circles of card punched with holes. Move the cups around then sniff the lids.

Which smells can you recognize?

Clean and dirty

You can smell if someone is clean or dirty. What would you smell like if you didn't wash for a week?

▲ When you do a lot of running or playing you can get very dirty.

You smell good when you have taken a bath and washed your hair.

Dirt with a bad smell is often full of germs that can make you sick.

What can you do to keep your home clean and smelling fresh?

▲ Cleaning makes things smell fresh and helps to get rid of germs.

◀ Bag up smelly garbage and throw it away.

Outdoor smells

I can smell hay and sheep.

We call the air outdoors **fresh air**.

I can smell fish and seaweed.

Smells in the country air, the sea air, and the city are very different.

I can smell traffic fumes and hot dogs.

You can tell where you are just by sniffing!

What else might you smell in the country, the beach, and in a city?

Indoor smells

The air inside your home is full of smells. There are different smells in each room.

What are the strongest smells in your home?

▲ Can you smell food and cooking in the kitchen?

◀ Can you smell shampoo and soap in the bathroom?

18

Sometimes you can tell what room you are in just by the smell.

Activity

Stand somewhere in your home. Close your eyes and ask someone to turn you around and around, so you don't know where you are.

Get them to lead you into different rooms. Give a good sniff. Does the smell tell you which room you are in?

Animals and smell

Animals use their sense of smell in all kinds of different ways.

◀ A mother deer can smell her own baby in a big herd.

▶ A shark sniffs blood in the water, then swims toward it to find food.

◀ A cat sniffs its food carefully before it eats it to make sure it is not bad.

Butterflies follow the smell of flowers to find **sweet** juice called nectar to drink.

Activity

- Collect petals of flowers with a sweet smell.
- Collect leaves of herbs such as mint and lavender.
- Lay them out on some paper to dry. Mix them together gently and put them in a bowl.

The **pot pourri** will make your room smell sweet.

INDIAN PRAIRIE PUBLIC LIBRARY
401 Plainfield Road
Darien, IL 60561

Glossary

Fresh air
We call the air outdoors
fresh air. You can open
a window to let fresh
air into a building.

Nose
Your nose is the part of your
body that you smell with.

Nostrils
The two holes in your nose
are your nostrils. Air goes
into your nostrils when you
breathe, and sniff.

Pot pourri
A mixture of sweet-smelling
petals and leaves.

Sniff
When you sniff, smells in
the air go up your nose.
You sniff when you want
to smell something.

Sweet
Flowers, fruit, and soap smell
sweet. Sweet smells are
usually nice smells.

Index

animals 9, 20–21

bad smells 5, 6–7, 10
beach 14, 15
blocked nose 10, 11
brain 8, 12

city 14, 15
clean people 14
cleaning 15
countryside 14, 15

dirt 14, 15
dogs 9

flowers 5, 21
food 7

fresh air 16, 22

garbage 15
germs 15

hearing 4
home 15, 18–19
hungry 7, 11

indoor smells 18–19

nice smells 5
nose 8, 10–11, 22
nostrils 8, 22

outdoor smells 16–17

pot pourri 21, 22

recognizing smells 13
remembering smells 12
rotten food 7

senses 4–5
sight 4
smell 4–5
smoke 6
sniff 8, 9, 13, 19, 20, 22
sweet smells 21, 22

taste 4
touch 4

warnings 6–7

Parents' and teachers' notes

- Talk about smelling things safely. Smoke and gases can be poisonous. Don't spray anything up your nose. Fine powders such as talc or pepper could damage your nose.

- Ask your child to draw a picture of their face smiling surrounded by pictures of smells that they like. They can also draw a picture of their face frowning, surrounded by smells they don't like. Talk about why they like some smells and dislike others.

- Make a smell chart. Collect drawings of things with smells that are sweet, delicious, disgusting, or give a warning. Sort and stick them onto four large sheets of paper. Make a collection of words to add to the pictures that describe how they smell.

- When you go out, encourage your child to notice and recognize smells in the air around him or her. Look at pictures of different places such as a farm, the beach, or a city. Talk about what you might smell in these places.

- You can learn new smells. Add a pinch of herbs and spices to drops of cooking oil (to stop the powder from going up your nose). Smell and name the different herbs and spices. Play a game to see which ones your child can match to the jars or containers they came from.

- Collect pictures of animals with different-shaped noses. Look for their nostrils. Discuss how they use their noses to breathe and smell.

- Ask the children to shut their eyes and smell different foods such as chocolate, orange, cheese, and honey. Can they tell what it is just by the smell? They can eat the food to check they got it right afterward!

- Discuss what it would be like if you couldn't smell anything. Talk about how it would affect your enjoyment of food. When would it be dangerous? When would you miss smelling? What would you be glad not to smell?